# You are a Social Detective!
## Explaining Social Thinking to Kids

WRITTEN BY:

MICHELLE GARCIA WINNER AND PAMELA CROOKE

ILLUSTRATED BY:

KELLY KNOPP

**You Are a Social Detective! Explaining Social Thinking to Kids**
Michelle Garcia Winner, Pamela Crooke
Graphic design: Elizabeth A. Blacker
Copyright © 2008 Think Social Publishing, Inc.

Social Thinking® and Superflex® are registered trademarks of Think Social Publishing, Inc.
Visit www.socialthinking.com for additional information on our trademarked and copyrighted
terms, and their use by others, including citation and proper attribution.

Library of Congress Control Number: 2008907978

ISBN: 978-0-9792922-6-2
062014

Think Social Publishing, Inc.
Social Thinking Publishing
3031 Tisch Way, Suite 800
San Jose, CA 95128
Tel: (877) 464-9278
Fax: (408) 557-8594

This book was printed and bound in Tennessee by Mighty Color.
Books may be ordered online at www.socialthinking.com.

Dedicated to all of the **Social Detectives**
we've worked with over the years.

## Dear Parent and Professional,

This comic book has many different concepts that can be reviewed over and over again with students. It is best to read this book in sections followed by real-life discussions with the kids about how the concepts apply to them personally.

The different sections include:

Enjoy watching your students and kids blossom into Social Detectives!

## AN IMPORTANT NOTE:

Please review the discussion of the use of the concept **uncomfortable thought** (weird thought) on page 54 before using this concept with your child/student. It is important we teach our students to notice their own thinking (good and uncomfortable thoughts about others) and that we don't use this term to just tell a student he is causing uncomfortable thoughts without strong related teachings!

## This isn't just a book for kids ...

Our hope is that it will be used as a way to introduce the concepts of Social Thinking to general education teachers, paraprofessionals, parents, caregivers, special educators, grandparents, siblings, day-care workers, scout leaders, etc., and of course, to those kids who are learning how to be Social Detectives!

Throughout the book you will see words that are highlighted in **bold lettering**. These are the key Social Thinking Vocabulary words that can be used in just about every environment by everyone. They are also the core Social Thinking Vocabulary words that are the basis for the lessons in the back of this book.

So, don't think you have to be a kid to enjoy learning about Social Thinking.

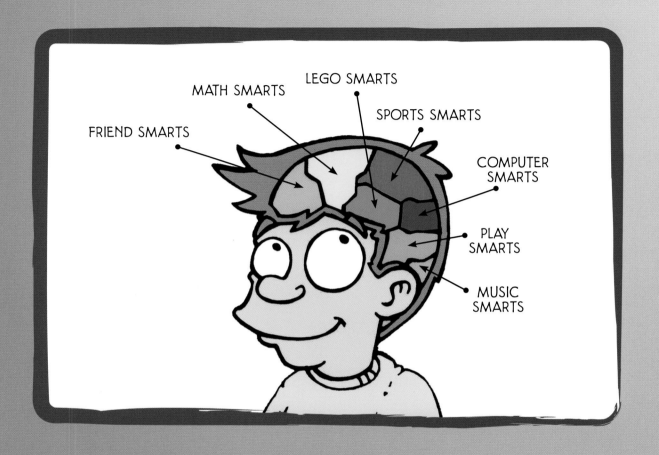

In our brains there are all types of "smarts." Some people have
really great computer smarts, music smarts, sports smarts, math smarts,
or even LEGO® smarts!

Everyone knows that we use **school smarts** at school, but
did you know we use our **social smarts** too?

We use our **social smarts** whenever we are around other people.

Using **social smarts** means understanding that others
have thoughts about us and we have thoughts about them even
when we are working at school.

4

We use our **social smarts** everywhere—NOT just in the classroom.
People think about each other in all different places.

One part of **social smarts** is knowing that kids think
about how other kids behave. We figure out how to behave based
on where we are and what we are expected to do at that time.

6

We think about whether kids are doing what is **expected**.
For example, we notice if other kids' brains and bodies are part of the group.

If their **body is part of the** group, then they are keeping their body close to other people in the group without touching others.

If their **brain is part of the group**, they are using their eyes to watch the teacher and others in the group. This shows they are thinking about what is happening in the group. They are **thinking with their eyes** to help them understand what is **expected**!

When we use our **social smarts**, it is expected that we play nicely
with other kids on the playground. That means that kids are saying
nice words to each other, letting others take turns,
and staying calm when someone else wins.

10

During group time in the classroom, we are **expected** to sit in the group, **listen with our eyes and our brains,** and do what the teacher asks us to do.

At nighttime we are **expected** to brush our teeth, put on our PJs, and go to bed when Mom or Dad tells us it's time to go.

No matter where we go ... when we do what is **expected**, people have **good thoughts** about us.

When people have **good thoughts** about us,
we feel good and others feel good about us too.

When people feel good, their faces are calm, their voices sound nice, and their bodies are calm. When people feel calm, they are more relaxed.

When a kid feels good, everyone enjoys being with that kid.
It makes playing or working together feel just right.

All of us like it when people treat us well. **But ...**

Sometimes people don't do what is **expected**!
When this happens it's called doing the **unexpected**.

18

We also think about whether kids are doing what is **unexpected**.
We notice when their **brain or body** is NOT a part of the group.
This means kids are doing their own thing and not looking
and thinking about others around them.

If a person's body is NOT a **part of the group**, then he or she is wandering away from the group or standing or sitting too close, which bothers others.

If their brain is NOT a **part of the group**, they are NOT **using their eyes** to think about the teacher and others in the group.
Instead, their eyes look away and that distracts their thinking.

On the playground when kids say mean words, don't take turns, or get very angry when someone else wins—that is **unexpected**.

During group time, if a student does not listen or pay attention
to the teacher and just does whatever he or she wants—that is **unexpected**.

At nighttime, if a child doesn't do what his or her parents ask—that is **unexpected**.

No matter where we go, when someone does something **unexpected**, people have **uncomfortable thoughts** about that person.

When people have **uncomfortable thoughts** about us, we don't feel so good about ourselves, and others don't feel great about us either.

When we don't feel good, we may not seem friendly.
We may use a mean-sounding voice or show an angry face.
Our body gets tight. This means we are upset.

When people have **uncomfortable thoughts**, everyone starts to feel unhappy. They may not want to play or work with the person that is making them upset.

Nobody likes to be with someone who is doing what is **unexpected** since it makes everyone feel bad.

SO ... to figure out what is **expected** in all the different places we play, learn, and go, we have to use our **social smarts**.

REMEMBER ... We all have **social smarts** in our brains.

When we use our **social smarts** well, we become **Social Detectives.**

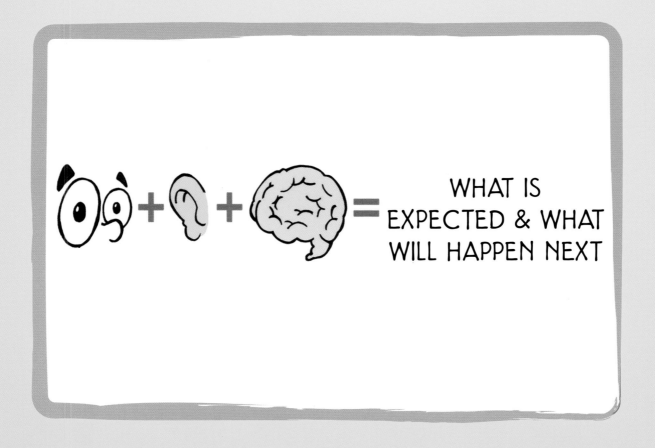

WHAT IS
EXPECTED & WHAT
WILL HAPPEN NEXT

**Social Detectives** use their eyes and ears along with what they know in their brains to figure out what is **expected** and even what may happen next.

With our eyes we can figure out what people might be feeling, thinking, or planning to do next.

With our ears we can figure out what people might be feeling, thinking, or planning to do next.

If we mix the thoughts we've collected from our eyes and our ears
and run them through our brain ...
TA-DAH!!!

We can figure out how to behave in all different places.

**Social Detectives** call this making a **Smart Guess!**

A **Smart Guess** is when we use all of our tools
(seeing, hearing, knowing, and feeling) to figure things out.

Take a look in the **Smart Guess** Toolbox to figure out the tools
that he is about ready to use! Do you have these tools too?

We make **smart guesses** all the time.
This happens in class, on the playground, and with our family.

Others make **smart guesses** about us too!
They try to figure out how we feel or what we are thinking.
For example, if we only use our eyes to look at books, then others
may make a **smart guess** that we are unfriendly because we are
not paying attention to others around us.

What kind of **smart guesses** do you want people to make about you??

If we forget to use our tools ... OOPS ... we might make a **wacky guess.**
No eyes + no ears + not thinking about what we know = **wacky guess.**

Look at the picture. Can you figure out what he's missing?
How will it change how he thinks about people around him?

42

An example of a **wacky guess** might be if you try to tell me something about me when you really don't know me.

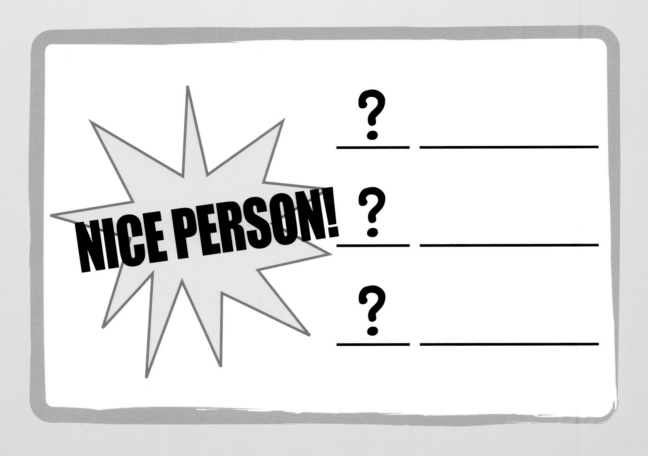

What are the **Social Detective** tools **YOU** use to figure out what someone wants to talk about or what they like to play?
Using these tools can help us figure out who we think is a nice person.

? _____ _____

? _____ _____

? _____ _____

What kinds of **Social Detective** tools do **YOU** use to figure out
if someone is not safe to play with or not nice to talk to?
Tip: A person is not safe to be around if they make you feel bad
with their words or how they treat you.

Being a **Social Detective** builds our **social smarts**.
This makes us better **Social Thinkers** over time.

Good **Social Thinkers** work well in groups, in the classroom, and on the playground.

SOCIAL SMARTS

SOCIAL THINKING ALL DAY

Can you be a **Social Detective** to build your **Social Smarts** all day?

Give examples of how you use your **Social Thinking**, even during math or when standing in line.

48

When good **Social Thinkers** grow up they work well with others in the office and in their homes—for example, as moms, dads, teachers, and other types of workers. Can you give other examples of how adults use their **Social Thinking** tools?

Now you can be an even better **Social Detective**.
People will feel good when you use your **Social Smarts** all day!!

# Social Thinking Vocabulary
for parents and teachers to use all day—everyday—
with their children and students.

**Note to parents and teachers:**
The following vocabulary and lessons are part of a larger social curriculum to help us all talk about social information and expectations more clearly. For more information about this topic, go to www.socialthinking.com.

# Social Thinking Vocabulary Definitions

From *Think Social! A Social Thinking Curriculum for School-Age Students* (Winner, 2005)

**Social Smarts:** The type of "smarts" in our brains that we use <u>whenever we are around other people</u>. Social smarts help our brains to know that others are having thoughts about us and we are having thoughts about them. We use social smarts in school, at home, and EVERYWHERE!

**School Smarts:** Different types of "smarts" in our brains that we use for school learning. Things like math smarts, computer smarts, music smarts, science smarts, and many more.

**Body in the group:** Your body is in the group if others feel you are part of the group. For example when you are standing, this means keeping your body about one arm's length away from others. The front of your body will be turned towards others in the group.

**Brain in the group:** Your brain is in the group when others feel that you are paying attention to what is happening in the group. For example, when you are thinking about others with your eyes and listening to what they are talking about.

**Thinking with your eyes:** This means that you are using your eyes to look at a person and it makes them feel that you are thinking about what they are saying or doing.

**Expected:** These are things we do and say that give people good thoughts about us and make them feel good too. Doing what is <u>expected</u> is different based on where we are and who we are with.

**Unexpected:** These are things we do and say that give people uncomfortable (odd) thoughts about us and make them feel icky or mad, or bad. Doing what is <u>unexpected</u> is different based on where we are and who we are with (different situations).

**Social Detective:** Every one of us <u>is</u> a Social Detective. We are good Social Detectives when we use our eyes, ears, and brains to figure out what others are planning to do next or are presently doing and what they mean by what they say and do.

**Good (okay or normal) thoughts:** Others have thoughts about us based on what we do and say. When a person has a good thought (normal thought) about us, it means that we figured out how to act in that place with that person. When others have good thoughts about us, they feel good too and may remember how we make them feel.

52

**Uncomfortable (weird) thoughts:** We have uncomfortable/weird thoughts about others and they have them about us, based on how people act, what people say, or how they physically present themselves. When a person has an uncomfortable or weird thought about us, it means we did some behavior that made people take notice of us in a more negative way, just like when we take notice of other's behaviors that make us have uncomfortable thoughts about them.

**SPECIAL NOTE ON THIS TERM:** *When working with students on this concept, it is ineffective teaching to simply tell the student others have uncomfortable or weird thoughts about them as a method of treatment. Instead the adults should use this concept to teach our students how they form "good thoughts" and "uncomfortable thoughts" about others and how this thought turns into an uncomfortable feeling about another person which impacts how they treat that person! Work with students to also recognize that people have uncomfortable/weird thoughts about everyone around them including adults, not just the student you are working with! NEVER tell a child he is "weird"; explain there is a difference between having an "uncomfortable thought" or "weird thought" and calling someone WEIRD! NEVER call a student a name thinking you are helping them; when people do this they are actually hurting a student far more than they are helping!*

**Smart Guess:** This is when we use all of our tools (remembering, seeing, hearing, knowing and feeling) to figure things out and then make a guess based on what we know about the world. Teachers also expect us to make smart guesses in class. Once they teach us information we are supposed to be able to use that information to guess what else might be needed or what might happen. Smart guesses are "expected" and make others have good thoughts about us because they know we are trying to figure things out!

**Wacky Guess:** This is when we forget or just don't use our tools (remembering, seeing, hearing, knowing and feeling) to figure things out.  Instead we just make a random guess without having any information. Teachers do not expect us to make "wacky guesses" in class or with our assignments.  Wacky guesses are "unexpected" and make others have uncomfortable thoughts.

**Social Detective Tools:** We all have social detective tools that we can use all of the time to help us figure out people and places.  These super important tools are:  Eyes and Ears and Brains and, of course, understanding feelings of others (sometimes people use a picture of a heart to represent that people have feelings).

**Social Thinker:** Each of us is a "social thinker" every day, each time we are around other people. It means we are always aware that people are around us and having thoughts about each of our behaviors. We are social thinkers, even when people are not talking to or playing with us. All of us should be social thinkers each day in a classroom. We can do this by being patient when someone else takes a turn or gives the same answer we were thinking about. Social thinkers know that we often share the same thought in a classroom when the teacher is teaching. Learning to become a better social thinker is what every person does their whole life!

It starts by working to build up that part in our brain called social smarts area. We can make that part of our brain get bigger by using the Social Detective tools.  The more we practice, the better our social smarts grow ... and then we can be an expert Social Thinker!!!

53

54

# Three Social Thinking Lessons

More lessons can be found in *Think Social! A Social Thinking Curriculum for School-Age Students* (Winner, 2005)

www.socialthinking.com

# Lesson: Expected and Unexpected Behavior in a Group
Adapted from the *Think Social!* Curriculum (Winner, 2005)

## Critical Vocabulary

Doing what is expected in the group
Doing what is unexpected in the group
"You can change my feelings."

## Tools & Materials

Poster of different emotions (optional)
Carpet squares or chairs

## What to Do

@ Once kids are in a group (on the floor in a circle or at a table), the teacher will perform a series of socially bizarre or "unexpected" behaviors (e.g., lie down on the floor, have your body turned out of the group, stand in the corner while talking, etc.).

@ Talk to the students about learning to be part of the group, but act as if you are just teaching them and nothing unexpected is happening.

@ Observe their reactions, but just continue and ignore their uncomfortable looks.

@ After a few minutes, ask the students if they think anything is wrong or odd about the way you are behaving.  Allow them to tell you how they "feel" about you doing these unexpected behaviors.

@ On the whiteboard, draw 2 columns and label the one on the left "Expected" Behaviors for the Group (draw a happy face) and the one on the right "Unexpected" Behaviors for the Group (draw a sad face).  This usually generates a really interesting discussion!

@ Using the students' feedback, write the behaviors on the chart that are unexpected in a classroom, such as lying on the floor, etc.

@ Write the expected behaviors for the classroom in the column on the left.

@ Talk about how they felt when you were doing unexpected behaviors.  You may have to help them by introducing a "feelings" poster or giving them terms such as "uncomfortable."  Talk about how they felt when you were doing expected behaviors (e.g., calm, okay, comfortable, normal).  Talk about how their feelings changed because of what you were doing.  Discuss how a person's behavior influences how they feel and how we are able to change how others think and feel about us based on how we change our behavior.

56

@ Have a discussion about what kids are supposed (expected) to do with their: eyes, head, shoulder, hands, feet, legs, mouth, etc. during group time.

@ Acknowledge the students for sharing how much they know about being in a group and how they are using their "social smarts" when figuring out what makes people feel good, okay, or uncomfortable when they are in a group together.

(This core concept of expected and unexpected is a critical concept upon which many of the lessons for Social Thinking are based. If you need more information, refer to www.socialthinking.com for a deeper discussion of other foundational concepts.)

# Lesson: Thinking with our Eyes

Adapted from the *Think Social!* Curriculum (Winner 2005)

## Critical Vocabulary

Think with our eyes
Thinking about what others are thinking

## Tools & Materials

None

## What to Do

⊚ Have the students close their eyes, and then give them vague instructions or ask questions like "look over there to see what is on the wall" or "who is that?"

⊚ Ask them what it is you are talking about with each question you ask.

⊚ Ask them to describe why they don't know.

⊚ Encourage them to realize they don't know what you are talking about because they can't see to what or to whom your comments refer.

⊚ Have them keep their eyes closed while you discuss this.

⊚ Have them open their eyes and introduce the language, Think with your Eyes.

⊚ Have them discuss how they use their eyes to think about what's in the room.

⊚ Introduce the idea that they can "think about what other people are thinking" if they "think with their eyes!"

⊚ Play a game where students try to guess what you are looking at based on the direction of your eyes. Then, play the game by having them guess what you are thinking about based on where you are looking. Start by looking at something very close to you (e.g., look at your watch or look right at them).

# Lesson: Social Spy or Social Detective
Adapted from the *Think Social!* Curriculum (Winner 2005)

## Critical Vocabulary

Be a Social Detective or Social Spy
Become a better observer and figure out others' plans
Reading others' plans by observing their actions (this is a simple way to teach children to read others' intentions)

## Tools & Materials

None

## What to Do

⍺ Brainstorm about what detectives do and encourage them to understand that good detectives have to observe people to try to figure out what they are doing, feeling, and what they are about to do next.

⍺ During this discussion, you should encourage them to think about others' motives/intentions.

⍺ Play the game: "Can you read my plan?"

⍺ Explain to the students that they can be "social detectives" and their job is to try to figure out what you are going to do next.

⍺ Teach students that they can think with their eyes and they can try to figure out your plan.

⍺ Encourage them to use their eyes, ears,  and brain to make a "smart guess" about figuring out someone's plan.

⍺ Start by doing something very obvious, such as reaching for a pen or reaching for the door handle, but stop short right before you touch the object and FREEZE. Hold your posture and see if they can guess what you were about to do. Many of your students can do this. You are teaching them to appreciate what their brains can already do and help them to learn that this is part of being a better "social thinker."

⍺ Have students take turns doing an action but stopping short of what they were about to do by freezing their bodies. Help them understand that they are not supposed to try to trick others but instead are engaging in teamwork.

◎ Once students get the idea of using their eyes, ears and brains to figure out others' plans, have them engage in more advanced group games like building blocks, LEGOs, or puzzles, as discussed in the *Think Social!* curriculum. Then you can explain how they can use their eyes to figure out not only others' plans but also how people FEEL about what they are doing!

◎ Teachers find that by breaking down these concepts, they open up a discussion with their students about the small steps of social behavior that are so important to running a classroom! In the past we have had little vocabulary for talking about social behavior; we have just expected students to behave! Now we have a way to talk to them. Enjoy your own creativity throughout this process.

Other ways to expand this activity can be found in *Think Social! A Social Thinking Curriculum for School-Age Children* (Winner 2005). The core concepts of Social Thinking are introduced in the book *Thinking About You Thinking About Me, 2nd Edition* (Winner 2007).

# Social Thinking® books, curriculum, thinksheets, and related products developed by Michelle Garcia Winner and Social Thinking Publishing

## Core Books About the Social Thinking Model and Curriculum
*Thinking About YOU Thinking About ME, 2nd Edition*
*Think Social! A Social Thinking Curriculum for School-Age Students*
*Inside Out: What Makes a Person with Social Cognitive Deficits Tick?*
*Social Behavior Mapping: Connecting Behavior, Emotions and Consequences Across the Day*
  *(also available in Spanish)*
*Why Teach Social Thinking?*

## For Early Learners
*The Incredible Flexible You™: A Social Thinking Curriculum for the Preschool and Early Elementary Years*
  *– co-authored by Ryan Hendrix, Kari Zweber Palmer, and Nancy Tarshis*
*We Can Make It Better! A Strategy to Motivate and Engage Young Learners in Social Problem-Solving Through*
  *Flexible Stories – by Elizabeth M. Delsandro*

## For School-Age Children
*You Are a Social Detective! – co-authored by Pamela Crooke (also available in French and Spanish)*
*Superflex... A Superhero Social Thinking Curriculum – co-authored by Stephanie Madrigal*
*Superflex Takes on Rock Brain and the Team of Unthinkables – by Stephanie Madrigal*
*Superflex Takes on Glassman and the Team of Unthinkables – co-authored by Stephanie Madrigal*
*Superflex Takes on Brain Eater and the Team of Unthinkables – co-authored by Stephanie Madrigal*
*Superflex Takes on One-Sided Sid, Un-Wonderer, and the Team of Unthinkables – co-authored by Stephanie Madrigal*
*Social Town Citizens Discover 82 New Unthinkables for Superflex to Outsmart! – co-edited by Stephanie Madrigal*